THE BEST ADVICE I EVER GOT

Business Today is India's No.1 business magazine with the highest total readership of all business magazines in the country. A product of liberalization, the magazine was founded in 1992 to chronicle the changing business topography of new India. Since then, it has set new benchmarks in both reportage-led stories and survey-led listings.

The Best Advice I Ever Got

THE BUSINESS TODAY TEAM

COLLINS BUSINESS

An Imprint of HarperCollins*Publishers*

First published in India in 2010 by Collins Business
An imprint of HarperCollins *Publishers* India
a joint venture with
The India Today Group

HarperCollins *Publishers*
A-53, Sector 57, Noida 201301, India
77-85 Fulham Palace Road, London W6 8JB, United Kingdom
Hazelton Lanes, 55 Avenue Road, Suite 2900, Toronto, Ontario M5R 3L2
and 1995 Markham Road, Scarborough, Ontario M1B 5M8, Canada
25 Ryde Road, Pymble, Sydney, NSW 2073, Australia
31 View Road, Glenfield, Auckland 10, New Zealand
10 East 53rd Street, New York NY 10022, USA

Typeset in 11/15.25 Dante MT
Inosoft Systems

Printed and bound at
Replika Press Pvt. Ltd.

Preface

During times of crisis such as the recent downturn, or even in the general milieu of tough competition that exists in the business world, what everybody, from the CEO to the *chaiwala,* welcomes is advice—some definitive words of wisdom from a person we personally admire and respect.

But advice turns golden only once it has been implemented and found to be of value in real life. For this very reason, *Business Today* decided to come out with a special issue in January 2009 that compiled the best guidance received by the super achievers of various fields. After the runaway success of the issue, we felt that such good counsel must not be limited to the short shelf life of a single magazine issue, and deserved to be made more widely available.

The Best Advice I Ever Got is, therefore, a compilation of good counsel that lent a hand in making the who's who of India's corporate world, as well as respected professionals and leaders from other fields, go from nobodies to people to reckon with. The book contains a few contributions we couldn't get in time to publish in *Business Today*; some have been modified or edited.

The diversity of the advice available in this selection is amazing. From the sublime to the practical, the advice is here for you to be inspired by and benefit from. So here's hoping that something you read here will one day feature in *your* list of 'the best advice I ever got'!

Rohit Saran
Editor
Business Today

Alok Kejriwal

Founder and CEO, Contests2win

The year was 2001 and the dot-com bubble had burst. Life was tough with 'Internet' becoming almost a bad word amongst the media and marketing community. As a start-up just into our second year, we had created a unique business model at contests2win.com but were finding it very hard to pull through the tough times. Since ICICI had invested in us just a year ago, as an entrepreneur struggling to make ends meet, I requested a meeting with Renuka Ramnath, the CEO of ICICI Venture, with the agenda of asking for more venture capital. I was granted that meeting almost immediately, and I presented Renuka a very passionate story of c2w and how we could create a great company if we received some more financing. It was a nice and well-packaged plea and Renuka heard me patiently. After I stopped speaking, she spoke, and her comment changed everything. She said, 'Alok, when we have children and they begin to walk, the parents help the child walk for the first few days and support it. Then one day, the parents stop supporting the child and expect it to walk on its own. It's difficult for the child and he/she craves for support from the parents, but that help doesn't come. The child falls, stumbles and even gets hurt but eventually learns to walk on its own since it has no alternative. In the same way, we believe it's time for you to find your own feet and be self-sufficient. It will be difficult… you will stumble and get hurt, but if you are determined enough, you will learn to support yourself. We cannot finance you any longer.' Renuka said no more, but what she had told me struck me like lightning. Something fundamental changed that moment… in the way I was thinking of my business. Rather than constantly looking for venture capital money to keep us going, I had to look at real-world finance in order to operate my business the way other businesses did. From 2001 onwards, Contests2win not only became a profitable business, but we also created three new companies—Mobile2win, Media2win and Games2win. We employed over 200 people and Mobile2win created value significant enough to be acquired by the Walt Disney Company in 2006.

Rashesh Shah

Founder Chairman and CEO, Edelweiss

There are two sets of advice which have stayed with me for a long time. In 1992-93, I and Venkat Ramaswamy were working with ICICI Bank. Because of our job profile, we often met Narayana Murthy, chief mentor of Infosys Technologies and our client at the bank. After our meetings, Murthy would often talk about entrepreneurship. In one of our interactions, he said, 'Always make sure your employees are your partners.' This advice has always stayed with us since then. It was an important piece of insight.

Again in 1995, when I and Venkat turned

entrepreneurs and started Edelweiss Capital, we met Narayana Murthy for advice. The Infosys campus had just become operational at that time. There are two things which he said and which have stayed with me since that meeting. One was when he said, 'Make sure you are profitable, otherwise you will share other people's dreams and not your own.' The other one was his suggestion that we should put the guiding principles and values of our company in writing, so that every employee can go through them and be inspired to follow them.

I am sure that in his long and illustrious career, he must have given advice to many people and may not have realized how important his advice was to the other person, but for us it became a core part of our value system. Whenever I happened to meet Mr Murthy while travelling, he would ask, 'Are you profitable?' and I would reply, 'Yes, we have been profitable year after year.'

That's how at Edelweiss we have built a strong culture of partnership where people think like owners. If an employee sees an AC running in an empty room, he feels that it's his responsibility to switch it off. It's not about retention and compensation only. It's about unleashing a culture of ownership among employees. Out of 1800 employees in Edelweiss, 800 have stock options and anyone who has spent two years in the company becomes eligible for stock options. We have also laid out the core guiding principles of the company in our annual report and a separate booklet is handed over to the new recruits and it's called 'your passport to Edelweiss'.

During the slowdown in 2001, Navtej S. Nandra, one of our board members and my senior from IIM Ahmedabad, pointed out that we should get our priorities right and remain focussed. When the going is slow, you can do hundreds of things and not achieve anything. So it really helped us during that tough period and remaining focussed is now an integral part of the company. Navtej was on our board from 1999 to 2003 and he helped us create balance scorecards to bring focus in everyone's role in the company. At the beginning of each year, senior employees create a Focus 10 (F10) list and they are measured against it on a quarterly basis.

I got another insight from Jim Collins' books *Good to Great* and *Built to Last* in which he analysed companies which did well over the years. I have learnt that if you constantly try to build a great organization, then everything else will follow. The market share, profitability, etc. will be taken care of.

One of these days, I and Venkat (executive director and co-founder) plan to meet Mr Murthy and thank him by presenting an annual report of our company to him.

—As told to *Rachna Monga*

Ramchandra Agarwal

Founder Chairman and MD,
Vishal Megamart

I imbibed the 'save more, spend less' ethos from my family which taught me that very single rupee matters. That focus on cost made sure that in the initial years when we had just a small shop and when Vishal Megamart was just starting out, we paid in cash for all goods purchased. Since we took no credit and bought in bulk, we got cheaper prices. It is a practice which we continued till recently. That put us on to our growth path. We hope to close the current financial at 40 per cent growth in topline at around Rs 1500 crore. Without this focus on the value of every single rupee, there would have been no business. Another advice that helped us grow was that of taking people along. Some of the members of the present team are the ones who have been with us for the last twenty years.

—As told to *Shalini S. Dagar*

Ashok Soota

Co-founder and Chairman,
MindTree Consulting

As a twelve-year-old schoolboy from the upscale La Martiniere in Lucknow, Ashok Soota got some sobering advice from his father. Days after making an impulsive and seemingly wasteful expenditure, Col. Ramlal Soota, an army doctor, gave his son some advice that the latter continues to use to this day. 'Don't waste money on a bargain purchase if you have no immediate use for it; instead, be willing to pay a little extra for a worthwhile deal,' he told his son. These words rang loud and clear for Ashok.

While his father's advice may have come some five decades ago, Ashok Soota has implemented the sage words in both his professional and personal life. For example, MindTree has made four acquisitions to grow its business over the last few years and Ashok heeded his father's advice on each occasion. 'We have walked away from perhaps the same number of deals as we've agreed to, due to pricing concerns,' says Soota. The same ground rules apply when he goes out shopping, albeit reluctantly. 'I don't like visiting malls or spending extravagantly on big brands... but on occasion I do spend on good deals,' he says.

—Written by *Rahul Sachitanand*

Karan Johar

Film Director

My Sindhi genes have just kicked in, otherwise I have always been an embodiment of *naam bada, darshan chhote*. All my films have been made on a commission basis, so the risk was entirely my own. But money was never really a big issue for me until I lost my father (producer Yash Johar) in 2004. Several things changed for me. My closest friend, Apurva Mehta, became my CEO and he told me to play the stock market as my father used to. He said it would be all right as long as I didn't become bullish about it. Then Shahrukh Khan told me that I better start leveraging my brand and that I should not be embarrassed about ensuring that I was paid for certain kinds of endorsements and appearances.

And then it was Aditya Chopra who sat me down one day and drew a diagram for me, saying there were three aspects to my life which I should compartmentalize: I was a film-maker, a creative producer and a brand that was up for endorsement. He told me that I should never do anything to compromise the master brand, because everything else is dependent on my making films.

There is, of course, my mother, who has always been telling me to invest in property—an advice that, I tell her, I can follow only if I have the money for it.

Nimesh Kampani

Founder Chairman, JM Financial

For me, my self-awareness and intuition have been the guiding forces in my life. But like everyone else, I have inherited my value systems and principles from my parents. My father followed these golden principles: never borrow money for personal needs and don't ever give guarantees. He would always say, 'The repayment liabilities are yours. You can't disown them. On the other hand, the asset which you believe belongs to you, may or may not remain of the same value. So the value of assets goes down but the liabilities stay with you.' Another way he would explain the concept to us was by saying, 'Liabilities are like a taxi meter which keeps running for twenty-four hours. The interest meter runs even when you go off to sleep. If you do business with your own money, you can tide over any bad phase. If you see what is happening in America, these principles are valid even today. As for benefiting from these principles, you can see the results in our company today—we have a net cash position.'

—As told to *Rachna Monga*

Shah Rukh Khan

Actor

There are two pieces of advice that Shah Rukh Khan says shaped his life and work. One was from his beloved (late) mother. She told him once: 'When doing your work, running a business or simply living your life, never think of reducing your expenses. Instead, think of ways to increase your income. The time and energy you spend on trying to plug holes, if they are spent on thinking of constructive ways to increase your income, will bear better results. It's also a more positive way of working.'

The other piece of wisdom he holds dear is from one of his oldest friends, actor-director Viveck Vaswani. Says King Khan, 'He told me: "When you start acting in movies, don't go by what films you want to be in, because you won't have much of a choice. First get to be in a position of choice and then do the films your heart desires. Become a star and then fulfil your artistic and storytelling instincts. Basically, deserve before you desire the roles you want."'

—Written by *Kaveree Bamzai*

Sanjay Nayar

Former CEO, Citi South Asia

There are two pieces of advice which I count among the best I ever received and which have significantly facilitated both my personal and professional growth.

The first piece of advice was from Victor Menezes, the former chairman of Citibank, who advised me on the opportunity to move back to Citi India in 2001 when I was comfortably settled in New York. To move from a developed, sophisticated capital market job and a place like New York to a promising emerging market, which India was then, was indeed a challenging idea. Victor outlined the advantages of moving to a market with enormous underlying potential, a diverse franchise and the opportunity to work across businesses, retail and institutional. In fact, his exact words to me, which now sound prophetic, were: 'This is the best job you will ever do.' Looking back, I can't but agree, as it has truly been a momentous and exciting journey over the last seven years: of opportunities, passion and tremendous growth in both my professional and personal life.

The second advice was received earlier, in the mid-1990s, from my father. Aware of my job in the UK and US, which required active involvement in the capital markets, he advised me to be prudent and risk-averse while managing personal savings. Coming from a middle class background, the focus for me was more on principal protection with expectations of modest returns. Accordingly, I made personal investments largely in bonds and FDs and continue to do so till date. As the past decade has shown, the returns from the debt markets in the US and fixed deposits in India have been more than satisfactory, giving me ample time to focus on my work.

—As told to *Rachna Monga*

Deepak Parekh

Chairman, HDFC Ltd

The best advice I ever got was from my uncle, the legendary Hasmukh Thakordas Parekh, when I was working with the US-based Chase Manhattan Bank in the mid-1970s. I was running around in New York, Hong Kong and Singapore, with stints with Ernst & Young, Grindlays Bank and Chase Manhattan Bank N.A.

I had spent nearly three years with Chase as assistant representative for south Asia when my uncle was stepping out to start his second innings, way back in 1977, after having worked with Industrial Credit and Investment Corporation of India (ICICI).

His idea was to set up a housing mortgage company for the middle class in India. Around that time, I had a good offer to go to Saudi Arabia to handle the Chase office there during the Middle East boom. In fact, my uncle was starting out a bit late in his life, at sixty, after retiring from ICICI, where he rose from being a general manager to the chairman. He asked me why I didn't settle down and work for a home-grown start-up rather than running around. He asked me to quit Chase and join him as deputy general manager. My uncle had a vision for a mortgage housing finance company—something not many thought about in the whole of Asia. I believed in his vision.

At thirty-four, I was married with kids at that time. It was actually a difficult decision since I had a cushy job with a foreign firm and life was also comfortable. My wife resisted my move to leave Chase, but I didn't heed her advice. I only had some initial concern whether it would work. Those days, I was at a fairly senior position at Chase and had to take a 50 per cent cut in my salary to join my uncle's company where there was no government or other funding support. I saw an opportunity in my uncle's vision and the job was also challenging, given the business environment. There were heavy regulations and people were also debt-averse. There was also no concept of housing finance. Even after joining, I never regretted my decision as the company had a good initial start. Though my uncle died a few years later, he saw that the company was moving in the right direction.

Today, when I see the world, it has changed a lot. The youngsters of today have to tread carefully. They have seen different phases of growth—the high and the low, and also the bull and the bear phase. One has to be very prudent while lending and stay away from complex derivatives products that they don't understand.

—As told to *Anand Adhikari*

Kalpana Morparia

CEO, JP Morgan India

The best advice I ever got was that I was 'too young' to give up my executive post. After I retired from the ICICI Group in 1997 as joint MD, there were a number of people within and outside the bank who kept advising me to come back in the executive post. It was a difficult decision then as I had worked for thirty-three years and was still engaged with the group as vice chairperson of the bank's non-banking subsidiaries in insurance, AMC and securities. It was like leaving your mother's home. But the executive role at JP Morgan Chase fitted well as it offered a huge opportunity to grow the business in India. We were not really impacted by the slowdown as we were at a foundation stage. There is a huge opportunity in this region as even after all downward revision, India was expected to grow at 5 to 6 per cent.

—As told to *Anand Adhikari*

Ashish Dhawan

Co-founder and Senior MD,
ChrysCapital Investment Advisors

If there is one advice that I have imbibed over the years, it is that it is important to have an independent mind when investing. The psychology of investing is often more important than the fundamentals of investing. It is important to be focussed on the basics and to be detached from what Warren Buffett calls 'Mr Market' and not be affected by market rumours and speculation. While Buffett has been a big influence over the years, exposure to people such as David F. Swensen and Robert Schiller in college had a seminal effect.

This advice was followed well while I was making my decision to invest in Shriram Transport. It was at a time when non-banking finance companies were hardly in favour with either the banks or the regulator, and investment in publicly listed companies was not popular either. The investment had great value proposition which others too saw, though at a later stage.

—As told to *Shalini S. Dagar*

Malvinder Mohan Singh

Group Chairman,
Religare and Fortis Healthcare

My father, the late Dr Parvinder Singh, has been a constant source of inspiration for me. He was a great visionary who believed in putting the company first, and whose advice was to be bold and to believe in your gut feeling. His words inspire me to think differently, take bold decisions and see them through.

In late 2007, I had my initial meetings with Daiichi Sankyo. At that time, our intention was to scout for a strategic partner. But as the talks evolved, it became clear to me that to realize the full potential of our vision, we would need to have a deeper relationship that would go beyond just a minority stake. On the one hand was the opportunity to clearly lead the agenda in terms of how the future dynamics of the global pharmaceutical industry would unfold. On the other hand, the only way we could do it was if our family was to sell its entire stake in the company in order to take the company to the next level of growth. If we went ahead, we would have the first-mover advantage, the opportunity to choose our partner, enter the deal on our terms and have the opportunity to create a pharmaceutical powerhouse. This would be the first time that a global generics company would be coming together with a leading innovator. Nothing like this had ever been attempted before. I decided to go with my gut feeling and took the bold step. In retrospect, it was a good decision. As it turns out, the environment has become tougher and other companies are being forced to consider similar deals. I believe ours was the game changer.

—As told to *Shalini S. Dagar*

G.V. Krishna Reddy

Chairman, GVK Group

I am as a person very aggressive and independent and prefer working in an economy where there is a free environment. This was one of the reasons why I opted to set up operations in the US during the Licence Raj era in India. Around the mid-1980s I was engaged in the manufacture of laminated particle boards in the US with operations in India. In 1990, M. Chenna Reddy, the chief minister of Andhra Pradesh then, happened to visit the US. He had come there for a kidney transplant and to invite NRIs to consider investing in his state and India, which was beginning to liberalize. I invited him to my factory in North Carolina and he quite liked it. He told me to leverage the opportunities that India now offered, particularly in the power sector. Over the next week, I studied the developments in India and talked to some of my friends and finally decided to come back and enter the power sector.

The third quarter of 1990 was a major milestone for us. That was when we bid for the Rs 817 crore Jegurupadu phase I power project and bagged it. It was the first independent power plant in the country and was operational by 1997.

Around that time, K.V. Kamath (MD and CEO of ICICI Bank), who has been my friend for 35 years, informed me that this was the time to get into the infrastructure sector in a big way in India, be it power, roads, ports, airports or telecom. I took his words seriously since I had known him to give sound advice, and acted accordingly!

—As told to *E. Kumar Sharma*

Deepak Puri

Chairman and MD, Moser Baer

The most profound advice came to me in 1983 or '84. Moser Baer, which was registered in 1983, was making time-keeping devices and I was looking to diversify into the world of computers. I was visiting my friend, Om Oberoi, the head of IDM (erstwhile IBM, which was thrown out of India by the Janata government) in Mumbai, asking him about the possibilities. As we were discussing that almost all manufacture related to computers required technology, he held up an 8"× 8" floppy disc and said, 'Why don't you make these?' I asked him for a defective piece as a sample and looked for some information about the manufacturers. It turned out that one of the companies was Xidex in the Bay Area of California where my brother was staying. My brother arranged for a meeting with the company in which I sought technology transfer from them and Moser Baer moved into IT manufacturing. After that, I have never looked back.

And my advice to myself is that if there is an agreement that is 60 per cent fair to you and 40 per cent to the other, then as soon as the other party gets one that offers a more equal share, he will walk out. It is important to be fair in life, in work and in relationships. That is the reason that Moser Baer has benefited immensely from its partnerships.

—As told to *Shalini S. Dagar*

M.V. Subbiah

Former Chairman, Murugappa Group

It was 1957 and I was studying mechanical engineering at the University of Birmingham, UK. Though I excelled in tennis there, the same could not be said about my subjects. Some time during my first year, my mechanical engineering teacher, Professor Mucklow, asked me why I wanted to be an engineer. After some thought, I said it was because my family was in the engineering business. Later, I took the exams and failed in a few papers. At the beginning of the second year, he called me over to his house for lunch and put forward the question to me again. I had not changed my views on the subject. Finally, as I was preparing for my second-year exams, he asked me whether I wanted to take the exams. By then, my marriage was fixed and I realized that aborting the engineering course midway would be embarrassing. He prodded me to realize my strengths. In the hostel comprising 150 students, of whom just 15 were foreign students, I had become the hostel representative. 'You are a man manager,' he said, adding, 'Do you want to be an engineer who gets paid Rs 250 a month or a top-class manager earning Rs 3000 a month?' Professor Mucklow further helped me discontinue engineering by arranging for me to do a two-year diploma in industrial administration (there was no MBA then). Apart from helping me understand my strengths, what impressed me was the way Professor Mucklow influenced me. He did not force his opinion on me. He kept track of me, let me run my course, and got me to take my own decision. He gave me a long rope. This style of functioning is something I diligently followed in order to nurture talent during my years at the Murugappa Group.

—As told to *N. Madhavan*

Azim Premji

Chairman, Wipro

It was 'standing-room only' for the keynote speech by Wipro Chairman Azim Premji at the TiE Entrepreneurial Summit 2008. For good reason too: Even though Wipro is majority-owned by the Premjis, the business is run very much like an entrepreneurial set-up, with 100 profit-and-loss units and the leader of each given a free hand.

The entrepreneurial spirit in him, according to Premji, was kindled by his mother, Gulbanoo M.H. Premji, when he was trying to transform Wipro from a struggling vegetable oil manufacturer to a technology and consumer goods company. 'Go against the grain and don't be afraid to listen to advice from across management. Some of the brightest advice comes from our most junior employees,' she said.

When Premji took over Wipro at the age of twenty-one, after his father's untimely death, the vegetable oil business was struggling and many people had written off the company. But he ventured into the almost-unheard-of IT industry. Later, when most of his peers stayed focussed on software services, Wipro entered the products business first and then expanded its domestic and Asia-Pacific operations. In Premji's case, his mother certainly knew best.

—Written by *Rahul Sachitanand*

Kiran Mazumdar-Shaw

Chairman and MD, Biocon

Soon after graduating from Bangalore's Mount Carmel College, Kiran Mazumdar followed thousands of others by taking medical college entrance exams. Despite her best efforts, Mazumdar failed to make the grade and found her life's dream of becoming a doctor shattered. Well before she made her name as India's biotech baroness and years prior to becoming India's richest woman, Mazumdar (before she married English businessman John Shaw and adopted his surname) found herself at the crossroads. She had always wanted to be a doctor, but her failure to enter medical school had dented these aspirations. At this crucial juncture, she turned for some sobering advice to her father, R.I. Mazumdar, a master brewer with UB. 'Every failure opens up a new vista. Learn to fight failure with a spirit of challenge. That will make you stronger,' he told Kiran. Rather than dwell on her setback, Kiran decided to turn to her love for the sciences, especially zoology and other biosciences, to try and become India's first female brewmaster instead.

Despite having the experience of her father to lean on, Kiran discovered an impenetrable glass ceiling in that industry too. 'A female brewmaster was unheard of in the industry at the time. Another door was slammed in my face,' she says. However she refused to cow down, depending instead on her academic skills and yet more sound guidance from her father. 'Remember that failure is temporary, it's giving up that's permanent. So, try and convert every failure into success and you won't feel like your world has come crashing down,' he told her.

The gender barrier meant that Kiran was twenty-four, fresh from an academic stint in Australia, and unemployed. Rather than fret about her future, she decided to take the challenge head on, cobbling together a small team of scientists and technicians and, persuaded by Leslie Auchincloss (founder of Biocon Biochemicals, Ireland) starting a business in Bangalore in 1978. That company, which started off by extracting enzymes from papaya, has today grown into Biocon, India's largest biotech firm. 'I would not have started Biocon had I not failed to get a job in a brewery,' she says.

—Written by *Rahul Sachitanand*

Piyush Pandey

Executive Chairman and Creative Director,
Ogilvy South Asia

In 1974, we were playing a cricket match against Hindu College. It was a crucial match for us and we were down 53 for 6. Arun Lal had just got out and I was entering the field. At that time, Arun told me something very important. He said, '53 for 6 is a problem for ordinary people but an opportunity for stars.' I remembered his words and concentrated on the game and made 71 runs in that match... and we won it. That's when I realized what Arun had told me... it simply meant 'in adversity lie opportunities'.

When Arun gave me this advice, we were facing

troubled times and I thought that it was just a motivational pep talk that he had given me. But this advice has helped me personally as well as professionally. I do not get perturbed easily and always look for an opportunity when adversity strikes. This approach has helped me come out of many a troubled situation.

My second advice came to me from my first managing director at Ogilvy & Mather India, S.R. Iyer. It was in the mid-1980s and I was three years old in the agency and was an accounts supervisor. Once in a while, Iyer would pick up one youngster and take him or her out for lunch and have a one-on-one chat on various things. It was my chance that day when he told me, 'Boy, take your *work* seriously but don't take *yourself* too seriously. That's the way of life. If you start taking yourself seriously, you will never enjoy life.'

This advice too has helped me a lot as it taught me to take each day as it comes and never hold back. Today when I look back at my career, I see that both these pieces of advice have helped me take the right decisions.

—Written by *Anusha Subramanian*

Shantanu Prakash

Executive Chairman and MD,
Educomp Solutions Ltd

The person who gave me the best advice I ever got does not wish to be named. The advice was to remain focussed during times of crisis and to use crises as opportunities to become stronger.

In times of crisis, first and foremost, create a distraction. This is because during crises, the focus shifts from looking at long-term organizational goals to immediate fire fighting. Not only that, the top management has to deal with uncertainties such as taking into account the possibility that the situation may become worse: the company may not get the loans it needs, or a regular customer may stop paying the company or may fail to do so, or suppliers may not deliver on time, and so on. This dissonance is tough to manage. In such times, even the most resilient of business minds are challenged to come up with a strategy that allows the business to navigate through the fear, uncertainty and doubt.

Challenging times need to be used as opportunities. The first thing to be done is to jettison all frills and wasteful activities. Times of prosperity induce a sense of complacency and can dull the sharpest of minds; so going back to the 'core' always brings clarity and focus. Secondly, increase investment in sales and marketing and build market share since your competitors are probably fighting their own battles and new competitors are unlikely to enter. Finally, force your mind to make choices and prioritize things. This again helps in gathering dispersed organizational energies to focus on the core products and services of the company.

I have used this advice time and again. In times of economic stress, I smile… and what could have been a challenge starts looking like an opportunity.

—As told to *Anand Adhikari*

N. Sankar

Chairman, Sanmar Group

The best advice I ever got was from my only boss, S. Ramaswamy, who was the general manager of Chemplast in the 1960s. After completing my education, I worked as his assistant to learn the business. He often told me that all management decisions ultimately boil down to common sense and logic. 'Most organizations get lost in all kinds of models and accepted practices, and logic is often forgotten,' he would say.

There was this one instance when we faced a troubling situation in Chemplast, the flagship company of the Sanmar Group. It was 2002 and alcohol, from which we produce ethylene dichloride (EDC)—our feedstock to manufacture polyvinyl chloride (PVC)—was in short supply due to higher demand from the potable alcohol sector and the gasohol programme. Volatile international prices made EDC imports costly. The only option was to set up a petrochemical cracker for sourcing ethylene to convert into EDC, but that would entail investing thousands of crores of rupees—something that Chemplast's balance sheet did not permit. We could import ethylene, but conventional wisdom was against it. Transporting this highly pressurized and volatile material by road to our plant located in landlocked Mettur (Tamil Nadu) was not advisable. We were in a fix and faced an uncertain future. Distancing ourselves from all that we were discussing, we looked at the issue through the prism of logic, and a solution emerged. Why not import ethylene by sea, convert it to EDC at a coastal facility and then transport EDC (a much safer product) by road to Mettur? In 2006, we implemented this plan. Had we gone with conventional wisdom, we probably would have been bankrupt by now.

Another piece of advice which Mr Ramaswamy gave me was in terms of letter writing. Although he was a chemist, he drafted English business correspondence beautifully. He told me that I should remember that whatever was conveyed by a letter was what the recipient understood in reading it, not what the writer *intended* to convey. His point being that the language should be clear, and not liable to be interpreted in many ways. I have found this advice very valuable when engaging in correspondence throughout my career.

—As told to *N. Madhavan*

Gautam Adani

Founder and Executive Chairman,
Adani Group

The corporate credo of the Adani Group is based on a piece of advice that even I do not know where it came from: 'When everything gets complicated and you feel overwhelmed, trust your intuition.' To elaborate on this, there are times when we find that we are caught in turbulent weather and see a maze of paths from which we have to get out.

My strategy to get out of the maze is three-pronged. Uppermost in my mind is survival—getting out of the maze, so to say—for which I trust my intuition to find the solution among the many possibilities that could work. After this, we at the Adani Group study the root cause of the problem and the signs or indicators that may forecast a similar problem resurfacing. Then we think about how we can put a plan in place to avoid such a contingency or adversity or, if it is not in our control, how we can fight it if it occurs again. Thirdly, we think out of the box, be as innovative as we can, and come up with ideas that take us forward from that point, with me trusting my team to implement the plan.

To give an example, we had identified a site for a jetty for a salt industry joint venture with Cargill which did not materialize. When the government opened up infrastructure development for the private sector in 1995, we entered the port sector since, being in the export business since 1988, we had realized that there was a lack of good port facilities in India. Thus, finding our way out of two problems—the site for the salt industry JV lying unutilized, and the limitations posed to our export business by port infrastructure shortages—we started the Mundra Port in 1998, despite the fact that the policy framework for concession agreement was still evolving when we commenced the construction of the port. The actual concession agreement was signed in 2001. So it was a calculated risk we had taken.

We had no experience in planning, developing or constructing a port. We managed to have a highly dedicated technical team which undertook construction in the marshy 'greenfield' site of Mundra, where only limited social infrastructure was available but which was highly feasible as a port because of its draught of about 17.5 metres and its location close to the north-western hinterlands, which account for much of India's import-export trade. Our business model for the port—the integrated landlord and terminal operator concept— was also unique. Usually, port activities are handled by a terminal operator and not the landlord port owner. It was difficult for us to recruit experienced personnel because human resource was simply not available for working on this kind of project.

We risked a lot of money and our reputation on the development of the port and have never regretted the project—India's largest privately handled port operation, handling about 30 million tons (mt) of cargo, and with expansion plans that include enclosed basin with about 16 berths in the next two years and, additionally, a dedicated coal terminal for the power sector coming up in the Kutch district. We want it to become one of the largest ports in the country, handling 50 mt of cargo annually by the year 2010 and 100 mt by 2015. With a first mover advantage in the port sector, we are now ready with India's first port-led SEZ.

—As told to *Anand Adhikari*

Javed Akhtar

Poet

This is something I have often said at school and college functions where I've been invited to speak. The best professional advice I ever got was when I was fifteen. I had just completed school from Aligarh and had gone to Delhi with my father, the poet Jan Nisar Akhtar, on my way to Bhopal, where I was going to Saifiya College. I remember that we went to visit my father's dear friend, Khwaja Ahmed Farooqi, who used to teach in Delhi University. He took us out for lunch and I remember him asking me: 'What do you want to be?' Now at fifteen, you think you can do anything and everything, so I gave him five or six alternatives. He then suggested that I should become a grass-cutter. You can imagine that I was somewhat startled by this piece of advice, but then he went on to say: 'But only on the condition that you become the best grass-cutter in the world, so that if the President of India wants the Rashtrapati Bhavan lawns to be trimmed, you should be the one person he thinks of.' He then said something which I will always remember: 'Koi kaam mamuli nahin hota, kaam karne wala mamuli hota hai (no work is insignificant, the worker may be). Whatever you do should be what you really want to do... joh tumhara dil chahta hai (what your heart desires). The security is in your excellence, not in the job.'

Chetan Maini

Co-founder and Deputy Chairman,
Reva Electric Car Company

Cars have been my passion throughout my life. As a child, I always tinkered around with remote-controlled cars. It is this irresistible love for cars which led me to car-centric universities in the US such as Michigan and Stanford. As a student, I spent more time making solar and hybrid electric cars than studying.

After completing my college education, I decided to work for a small start-up company that specialized in electric vehicle technology. I could have joined our profitable family business of making automotive components or taken up other private jobs which offered huge salaries. But that was not where my heart lay.

My father, Dr Sudarshan Maini, too nurtured my ambitions when he said very clearly, 'Do what you really love doing and give nothing less than 200 per cent.' I have always gone by this advice. Throughout my life, work has never been 'work' for me; instead, it has been a passion. This led me to start Reva Electric Car Company and has shaped me into what I am today. My father, who is a first-generation entrepreneur, has always had enormous faith in himself and often took huge risks in life. I have learnt a great deal from him through a combination of his advice and actions.

—As told to *K.R. Balasubramanyam*

Aamir Khan

Actor

I think I was around fourteen when during the course of a conversation with my uncle Nasser Hussain, he told me to follow my heart... and those words have stayed with me ever since. 'Quite often in life,' he said, 'you are faced with situations where you may go wrong, but even so, if you follow your heart, it's always better to go wrong on your own instincts than on anybody else's.'

I believe that following this advice has been instrumental in my choice of profession, particularly since many of my well-wishers were set against it. Their fear was not entirely unfounded. At that time, completing your studies was considered paramount and they wanted me to have some option to fall back on in case I didn't succeed in tinseltown, whereas I was very clear that I wanted to dive right into film-making and acting rather than study commerce, which I was doing at that time.

Since then, most of my decisions have been based on this philosophy of trusting my instincts. Though, there have been times when I have been wrong, to be more specific, in terms of my choice of movies. It's impossible to say what would have happened had I not listened to my uncle's words of wisdom or not got this piece of advice from him. I am an independent person with my own thought process, so I believe I would have followed my heart, even if those golden words hadn't come from my uncle; though I must add that they *did* help me focus my energies on my goal. His words set me on the path of figuring out my own way. Whether things went right or wrong, it was the path of my choosing and my mistakes to live and learn from. That's exactly what I advise my nephew, Imran.

—As told to *Tejeesh N.S. Behl*

Jamshed J. Irani

Director, Tata Sons

I left home at sixteen to study abroad. As a child, I was very close to my father, who was also an executive with a Tata company. He was the best mentor I had and he told me something that is ingrained in me: 'Son, out of every ten men who are born in this world, nine work for the tenth. So prepare yourself to be the tenth.' These inspiring words enabled me to plan my future as a leader. This piece of advice also enabled me to think about how to get the best of the other nine.

If you want to make an impression on the world, you need an army behind you. Politicians, corporate leaders and even Nobel laureates have an army working for them. Leaders must have that credibility which enables their legions to follow them to achieve anything. You have to be a leader all the time and can't switch off at any point. You can't say that you will switch off and sleep through the night and be a leader in the morning.

I believe you must form a team and be with your army. If you are too far ahead of the army, you will get cut off. It's only as a team that you can succeed. To be a leader, you have to get the team behind you, and that has always been my motto throughout. You must always be aware of your responsibilities as a leader, even under pressure. You must never allow your discomfiture or your inability to take a decision to show since that may prove disastrous. If a captain were to tell his team: 'Guys, we can't score the total on the board. Forget it! Do what you can, but I don't think we can chase that figure,' it would be a disaster. A leader, however he may feel inside, must say that the goal can be achieved, and achieved well, and the team will follow.

—As told to *Clifford Alvares*

G. Madhavan Nair

Chairman, Space Commission

The best advice I ever got was during the late 1960s, from our beloved Dr A.P.J. Abdul Kalam with whom I had worked almost all my career. He told me that when we handle major projects where complex technical issues are to be solved, the contribution made by each individual in the team counts. He believed that, in all our tasks, we must involve even those who may be not be rated as high performers but can contribute their best and eventually lead to the success of the project. This advice has held me in good stead while I led major projects such as the Polar Satellite Launch Vehicle (PSLV) project as Director of Liquid Propulsion System Centre and Vikram Sarabhai Space Centre, both in Thiruvananthapuram. The result of his advice is evident from the success of Chandrayaan-I too.

When you lead an organization, the leader should take everyone along and ensure that each person gets an opportunity to give his best, and that he be given the credit for it. 'A leader,' Dr Kalam said, 'should always lead from the front.' If a project is successful, then its leader must share the credit with all the members of his team. However, if it runs into trouble, then the leader must take the responsibility. Dr Kalam's advice always rings in my ears and has been the guiding spirit in my professional life.

—As told to *K.R. Balasubramanyam*

Akhil Gupta

Senior MD and Chairman, Blackstone

In 1974, when Dr Ashok Ganguly was the general factory manager of the Garden Reach factory of Hindustan Lever in Calcutta and I was a management trainee, there was a strike by the workers and we were stranded inside the factory for forty-eight hours. I was criticizing the workers when Dr Ganguly, who would later become chairman of HLL, said, 'Every problem can be traced back to failure of management and leadership.' That was such a powerful lesson that I have applied it in all spheres of my life. As a responsible person, you don't look for excuses or find people or situations to blame, but focus on what *you* can do to achieve the desired results.

—As told to *Shamni Pande*

Venu Srinivasan

Chairman and MD, TVS Motors Ltd

I have received much advice that has had a profound impact on me. My friend and philosopher, Prof. Lord S.K. Bhattacharyya, head of Warwick Manufacturing Group, University of Warwick, UK, has had an enormous influence on my growth as a business leader over the last thirty years. His advice: Never take more than one risk at a time. He classifies risks into people, markets and money—the three legs of a tripod. If you take more than one risk, the tripod loses balance. For instance, he would say that a financial risk such as an acquisition can be attempted successfully only if you have a strong team and a stable market. His contribution and support have had a far-reaching impact on the product-development capacity and strategic thinking of TVS Motor Company.

In the early part of my life, my father and uncles played an important role in teaching me the TVS values: trust, integrity, discipline. People would set their clock depending on the arrival of the buses run by the TVS group, they would say, highlighting the importance the family gave to discipline and punctuality. Ramnath Goenka, whom I had known from childhood, helped me understand the social and political milieu in which we operate. He often said, 'Venture into areas which you can handle coming from the TVS family.'

In the early stages of my professional career, Professor Washio and Professor Tsuda, Japanese TQM (Total Quality Management) experts, revealed the importance of building a TQM organization that fits in with the times. Without their advice, we could not have built an organization that had excellent people and processes and which upheld 'the TVS way' effectively.

—As told to *N. Madhavan*

G.M. Rao

Founder Chairman, GMR Group

I started my entrepreneurial venture through a small trading business. Simultaneously, I got engaged in the running of a jute mill. In those days, businesses were primarily driven by Licence Raj. My friend, an astute banker working in that area, advised me to stay focussed on one category of business. I took his advice and chose to focus on the running of the jute mill, leaving the trading business to my brothers.

From then on, I stayed focussed, prioritized issues, and avoided procrastinating. This has helped the GMR Group to successfully complete challenging projects ahead of schedule and to set the benchmark in many a project.

I must say in all humility that these qualities have helped us build GMR from a small jute mill to a major infrastructure developer, presently executing the challenging task of setting up the international airport in New Delhi, which will be the second largest terminal building in the world.

—As told to *K.R. Balasubramanyam*

G.V. Prasad

Vice Chairman and CEO,
Dr Reddy's Laboratories

One's early influences are often the most profound. This is certainly true in my case. The best advice I have ever been given was by my mother, G. Syamala, who taught me to always raise the bar and never be content with the status quo. Though my mother was not able to complete her schooling, she placed a tremendous value on education. It was she who pushed me to excel and perform beyond my own expectations.

In Class VIII, I was a reasonably good student and was quite satisfied with myself. My mother, however, wanted me to stand first. She encouraged me to raise my aspirations. By the time I reached Class X, I had worked my way up to the top of the class. This taught me that there are no limits to what one can achieve.

The advice to 'think big' became an intrinsic part of my make-up and approach to corporate life. I have extremely high aspirations for the organization and its people. In virtually every sphere, be it performance, corporate governance, HR, quality, or safety and health, we were ahead of our peers in the Indian pharmaceutical industry in implementing the best policies and practices. A favourite quote of mine is by Bernard Shaw, who said, 'Satisfaction is death'. I strongly believe that we must never be satisfied with what we have achieved, but must continually strive to improve.

I have also absorbed valuable lessons from other remarkable members of my family. My father is a very detail-oriented person, whereas my father-in-law, Dr Anji Reddy, is a 'big picture' person and a visionary. From him, I learnt to look at the forest, and from my father, to look at the trees. So I have the unique advantage of being able to see the trees as well as the forest. Because of this ambidextrous capability, I am able to look into the long-term needs of the organization and simultaneously focus on its immediate priorities.

In the early 1990s, when we were still a mid-sized company, I championed our entry into the North American generics market, envisaging that it would make us a serious player on the global generics stage. At the same time, we were implementing a number of important initiatives on the ground to improve processes and systems, the building blocks of the business as it were. And these were in place to support and sustain our growth into a $1 billion company.

Finally, I learnt a very important lesson in leadership from Mahatma Gandhi, who had the ability to communicate great ideas in a very simple way. He said, 'Be the change you want to see in the world.' I regard this as a call to lead by example and expect from myself the same standards that I expect from others. I know that if I want others to follow, I must be prepared to go first.

—As told to *E. Kumar Sharma*

Harsh Mariwala

Chairman and MD, Marico India

If I look back and think, there is no single advice I would like to separate from the numerous words of advice I have received. But if I have to do so, I would probably say it is about 'investing in people and empowering them'. This advice has come to me in various ways, from various people, and has been critical to my success as an entrepreneur.

I have learnt that it is only by investing in the right people that innovations happen. And this is something which has got reinforced over a period of time and is one of the cornerstones for the success of Marico. When I first started Marico, there was no capital investment and we only had unbranded products. Slowly and steadily, when we started investing in people and innovation, the business got transformed.

I learnt a lot about dealing with people during my battle with union leader Datta Samant. It's during this battle and the negotiations with him that I realized how important it was to have a win-win relationship in negotiations so that you achieved what you wanted for the benefit of all. Personally and professionally, the experience helped me to become more understanding and flexible while dealing with people. This is also a culture that I have inculcated in my organization.

Prof. Ram Charan is another person whose writings and teachings I follow keenly. An important piece of advice I got from him was during the mid-1990s when I was fighting it out with Hindustan Lever, which was trying to buy us out. That's when Professor Charan told me, 'Come what may, you need to protect your resource-generating engine.' Our resource-generating engine was the Parachute brand. Those words gave me a lot of courage to fight the battle with Levers and we ultimately succeed in keeping the company and brand with us.

—As told to *Anusha Subramanian*

Shelly Lazarus

Chairman, Ogilvy & Mather Worldwide

The best advice I have ever got was from our legendary founder, David Ogilvy. Just before becoming the CEO of this company, I spent three days with him at his château in France. We spent most of our time discussing and talking business. As we were talking at one point, I asked him what he would say to me if he could give me just one advice. And he said, 'Just pay attention to your people. That's the most important thing you need to do. No matter how much time you spend thinking about, worrying about, focussing on, questioning the value of, and evaluating people, it won't be enough. If your people are happy, and feel successful, they will be productive and everything else will work well. People are the only thing that matters, and the only thing you should think about.'

Then he cited his own example and said, 'When I founded this company and was running the operations, I spent all my time thinking about just one thing, and that's my people... and I still feel that it is not enough.'

As a result of this advice, I spend some amount of time every day, asking myself, 'Am I doing enough? Are my people happy? Is there something I need to do which I am not doing?'

David's advice is very simple and tackles the fundamental issue—people. It drives not only how I think about and mentor people, but also how I form business strategies and take critical decisions. In the field of advertising, ideas don't materialize out of thin air but from people, and at O&M we have brilliant minds that come up with great ideas. I feel lucky that he believed in me and found me deserving enough to give me this advice.

—As told to *Anusha Subramanian*

Raghav Bahl

Founder and MD,
Network 18 Group

Here is the best advice I've ever got: 'Surround yourself with the best people and set them free. Trust them, empower them and lead by example. People are suckers for respect.'

—As told to *Shamni Pande*

M. Rammohan Rao

Former Dean, Indian School of Business

In late 1969 as I was completing my thesis (on multi-commodity warehousing models in the area of industrial administration), I was talking to my professor, W.W. Cooper, who taught accounting and operations at the Carnegie-Mellon University, about career options and in the context of what I wanted to do and on things like why, despite competence, many people still do not seem to make it. It was then that he told me something that I still value: 'Competence alone is not enough. In addition, one needs an ability to convince others and be confident without being arrogant.' What he said then holds true even today. One sees many competent people but the way they behave puts people off and, because of this, they do not necessarily get the recognition that they should be getting.

The advice helped in giving me a different perspective and one that is not narrowly focussed. It helped me broaden my interests and look at other areas of work, research, teaching and learning. Today I say this to my students too, and my pet line is that the dividing line between confidence and arrogance is very thin. You should appear to be confident, but not arrogant.

—As told to *E. Kumar Sharma*

Prasoon Joshi

Chairman, McCann Worldgroup India

I have got several pieces of advice from people at various stages of my life. But if I have to zero in on one, it would be the one which my father gave me very early in life when I was just a ten-year-old. He read out a particular verse for me from the book *Kathopanishad* which talks of *shreya marg* and *preya marg*. Explaining the concepts, my father said, 'There is a path which is beautiful and there is one which is difficult. But, you must always take the path that is difficult because the difficult path leads you to your destination and the beautiful path is a destination in itself.' He himself believed strongly in this statement.

I took this advice seriously and have always chosen the difficult path as opposed to an easier or more beautiful path in whatever I am doing. It takes a lot of courage to do so but I can tell you that I have never been disappointed with my decisions, whether it be in personal or professional life.

Another advice I take very seriously is one that was given to me by A.R. Rahman, the music director. This was when I first worked with him, on the music of *Rang De Basanti*. While chatting and talking about our previous work, he told me: 'Believe in the present and do justice to it.' What he meant was that instead of pondering over the past and trying to figure out what went wrong, it is always better to concentrate on the work to be done at present and to try and do that well. That's precisely what I do. I concentrate on the present and try and do a good job of it.

—As told to *Anusha Subramanian*

William P. Lauder

CEO, Estée Lauder

When I was still a young student at Wharton Business School, I got an opportunity in the summer of 1982 to work with Donald Regan, then the US Secretary of the Treasury under President Reagan. I was used to working in office since, every summer prior to this job, I had worked at Estée Lauder companies. My job title at Donald Regan's office was 'special assistant to the special assistant'—something that I had not anticipated.

The first day of my job, I realized that I was in a high-profile job at the age of twenty-two—a fact that kept me on my toes all the time. When I finally met Regan alone, I was presenting an energy pipeline policy memo to the treasury secretary of the United States. Regan, who was the previous head of Merrill Lynch and a former marine, had a direct, and directive, style. Marching into one of our meetings two minutes early (unusual for a politician), he glared at his watch and then at me. 'Lauder!' he bellowed, 'I give this advice to all my reports: If you're not in control of your calendar, you're not in control! If anybody else controls your calendar, you are going to be a victim and are not going to be in control of what you do.'

I have always taken this advice very seriously and ensure that I know what I am doing where, when, why and with whom, so that I do not continually say 'yes' to everything and I am able to do things more effectively. The advice, however simple it may sound, has been very valuable for me to this day and has helped shape our company's unique strategy, how I manage myself, and my philosophy. Time is our greatest resource, and when it's gone, it's lost forever.

—Written by *Anusha Subramanian*

R.C. Bhargava

Chairman, Maruti Suzuki

I believe the aging process slows down if a person keeps learning even when he gets 'old'. Age should be no bar in doing new activities, or doing things in new ways.

Before starting a career, learning is mainly done through academics. Thereafter, one learns at the workplace, undergoes various training courses, listens to lectures by people who are more learned and experienced, interacts with persons who have greater knowledge, and gains more insight into life and the world by reading books. These are all, in a broad sense, 'advice' which shape one's personality and ability to add value to one's employer and to society.

Choosing the most valuable advice I ever received is difficult since there is a lot of advice that I have received and found valuable enough to listen to and profit from.

Should it be the lesson from the *Gita*, that one should strive to do one's duty to the best of one's ability, but not worry about the results as they are never fully in one's control—a lesson that enabled me to remain focussed on my work during difficult times? Or Sathya Sai Baba's words that one should strive to help rather than hurt others—words that led to better decision making and led to a sharper focus on looking after consumer interests? I also learnt a great deal from the Japanese, which helped in taking Maruti to the heights it has scaled.

However, the most valuable advice I ever received was probably given by a person whose name I do not even remember now. In the days when I was freshly out of the university, and was a trainee in the IAS, I was told that in my career I would be posted in diverse jobs and would have to learn about these new areas in a short span of time. I would also have to seek the cooperation of technocrats who had much longer experience of work than I had. The best way of achieving both objectives would be to say, 'I don't know, please tell me,' in respect of as many topics as possible.

This piece of advice to accept it humbly if I did not know about something actually worked wonders. I learnt far more than I could have ever done from files, and also won the cooperation of others in the department. Thus in the energy ministry I was taught by many engineers about the electricity industry and Mr Tata Rao, the chairman of the Central Electricity Authority and a doyen amongst power engineers, paid a very high compliment by writing to me as Er R.C. Bhargava! (In the earlier days, there was antagonism between bureaucrats and technocrats, particularly engineers. He was thus paying me a high compliment by prefixing Er, abbreviation for engineer, before my name.) The same words helped me when I joined Maruti with virtually zero knowledge of that industry. I wish I could remember who gave me this valuable advice which gave me a jump-start and enhanced my ability to learn, and produce better results.

Vikram Akula

Chairman, SKS Microfinance

When I started working in the field of development, I held the view that the poor were ignorant and uneducated. I imagined that I would help teach the poor how to improve their lives. I would learn modern agricultural techniques and become versed in scientific dairy farming procedures and impart this knowledge to the poor. Most people admired and lauded my aspiration to bring modernity to the ignorant masses… but not Biksham Gujja.

Biksham was my first boss, the Director of an NGO, the Deccan Development Society. 'Well, you know, you really can't help the poor. They know a lot more than we do,' he said to me one day. I was puzzled by this statement, but wrote off his response as simply an attempt to show outward humility. Surely, he did not really believe that the poor knew more than us—the modern, progressive segment of society. Surely, *we* had to educate them, not the other way around. So, despite Biksham's words, I started my work, driven by the notion that I was going to help the poor.

But I soon saw what happened when the 'educated' tried to 'help' the poor. I saw how bureaucrats gave subsidized loans for high-yielding buffaloes and how these buffaloes died in tough drought conditions, leaving the poor worse off. I saw how the introduction of capital-intensive agriculture actually led to water tables falling. So, while a handful of farmers benefited, the rest of the community suffered. I saw how education failed to prepare rural children to get a job, yet succeeded in alienating them from their traditional economies, leaving them neither here nor there.

I realized that Biksham was right. I had to

abandon my notions of helping and really listen to the poor. I put away my books and immersed myself in the rhythms of Indian villages. I drank *chai* in village stalls, ate in roadside *dhabas*, travelled on rural buses, and stayed in the huts of the poor, all the while talking informally and learning from the poor. I used participatory techniques to enable even the illiterate to illustrate their ideas—using stones, flowers, sticks, and chalk powder. By listening to the poor, I was able to understand their lives and hear their ideas, which allowed me to help design programs that worked.

The idea that the poor are not ignorant but have knowledge and ideas about how to change things is a lesson that I carried with me when I started SKS Microfinance, which today provides financial services to over 3.5 million poor households. Rather than using 'experts' to design products and processes, I listened to the poor. I asked villagers to show me their seasonal cash flow needs using sticks, seeds, and coins. I encouraged them to use coloured chalk powder and flowers to map out the village on the ground, thus indirectly telling me where the poorest people lived, what kind of financial products they needed, and so on.

Using these inputs, I designed a set of products and processes specifically for the poor. For example, based on visual exercises about how money ebbed and flowed from households—when pay day was, what financial crises families faced, etc.—I set our weekly repayments at as low as Rs 50 per week and our retail and health insurance premiums at Rs 20 a week and Rs 500 per year.

This approach resulted in a system that worked for the poor, making SKS one of the most successful microfinance companies in the world.

—As told to *E. Kumar Sharma*

Kishore Biyani

Founder and CEO, Future Group

I believe some of the best advice I ever received was unspoken. I never had mentors who would provide sagely advice. Instead, I sought advice and insights from reading books and plain observation. The most decisive advice I gathered came from watching a store in Chennai's Ranganathan Street.

In the year 2000, we were working on the idea of starting a retail chain that would sell, at a discounted price, almost all kinds of merchandise that an Indian household consumed. I would meet a lot of people, discuss the idea with them and use them as a sounding board. There was one set of people, mostly consultants, who would say, 'It's a hypermarket model. You've got to study how these hypermarkets work in the US and Europe.' I had then hardly travelled abroad and couldn't relate to what they proposed.

There was another group of people, mostly local businessmen, who would be sceptical about the idea. At that time, there were hardly any large-format stores in India and this group would say that such a business model wouldn't work here.

That's when I came across Saravana Store in Chennai. Standing outside the store I noticed that hordes of people would walk into this store spread across five floors and a basement, at any time of the day. It stocked everything—from appliances to grocery to clothes, jewellery, toys and even eyeglasses. For many, Saravana may be a shopper's nightmare, but there were a lot of customers who just loved it and demonstrated their approval with their frequent footfalls. Saravana served as a template to build upon the idea of Big Bazaar. We developed a model that could be replicated and turned into a pan-Indian chain. The idea worked for us.

Down the years, some of the best advice for Big Bazaar has often come from just watching our customers and how they behave. Every small or big decision a customer makes inside the store, every story he or she communicates, explicitly or otherwise, is considered a valuable piece of advice.

—As told to *Anusha Subramanian*

Gurcharan Das

Author, former CEO, P&G India;
former MD, P&G Worldwide
(Strategic Planning)

Our family moved to Washington DC in the mid-1950s when I was thirteen. The Indian government had posted my father there as a part of a small team of engineers to negotiate the division of the rivers of the Punjab with Pakistan, under the mediation of the World Bank. We arrived in America during the heyday of the Eisenhower age, and the country was in the midst of unparalleled prosperity. The American middle class was absorbed in the serious business of collecting bigger appliances and bigger cars for its bigger homes in the mushrooming suburbs. I was put into a typical American high school which was a short bus ride away from our home on 18th Street.

One day our neighbour advised my father that I ought to get a 'paper route'. And so, like millions of American kids, I got a job delivering newspapers before school. Each morning I would walk down my route, delivering the *Washington Post* from house to house. I had to get up at 5 a.m. In the freezing cold of winter, that required a lot of will power. But I knew that my customers depended on me. There were other things that I had to bear in mind too—when it rained or snowed, I had to cover the newspapers so that people didn't have to struggle with wet pages. I had to hold my tongue even if they did not pay me on time. My paper route taught me that the customer was the most important person in America. No matter how big you were, you had a customer.

I also learned that America was truly the land of opportunity. Not only because there were jobs available, but because a hard-working person could hope to rise to the top in every field. Almost everyone believed that the best person would get ahead. Americans were positive and optimistic. They did not think, as we did in India, that you had to snatch something from your neighbour in order to succeed. Both could get ahead, as there was enough to go around.

In my school in Washington I was surprised that we had to attend a class called 'shop'—a classroom which was filled with lathes, tools, and machines, and we learned to work with our hands. We learned to repair a house, a car, or a radio. We could make a table or unclog a sink. At the end of the year, we had lost our fear of technology. We had understood Bronowski's dictum that the world is understood through the hand, not the mind—the hand is the cutting edge of the mind. Some of us became 'tinkerers'. This is a powerful idea for India where we have traditionally had contempt for manual labour. It goes back to our caste system. The lowest caste *shudras* were denied knowledge and worked with their hands while the three higher castes worked with their heads. Hence, we do not produce tinkerers in India. A tinkerer combines knowledge with manual labour, and thus you get innovation. Our entrepreneurs, who come from the upper castes, are not innovators partly because they are shy of technology. This may be one of the reasons why we failed to create an industrial revolution in India.

Anu Aga

Director, Thermax

I have amalgamated inputs from several people through the course of my life, starting with my parents, my husband and even from my children. From my mother, I learnt to be authentic and not to pretend, which came in handy when I took over as Chairperson after my husband's (Thermax founder Rohinton Aga) demise. I didn't know anything about the business and admitted as much to the senior management when I sought their help in running the company. My father advised me to invest in myself and to live within my means, which is a philosophy we follow at Thermax where we'd rather be understated than ostentatious. From my husband, I learnt not to be afraid and to have meaningful relationships... though, of course, not all relationships can be meaningful. I owe my involvement with Thermax's corporate social responsibility initiatives to my son, Kurush's (who died in an accident) advice. My daughter (Meher Pudumjee, chairperson, Thermax) taught me to accept people for who they are rather than trying to mould them into what I wanted them to be. Of course, this applies to inter-personal relationships and not to business dealings where you need to be demanding—a trait I inherited from my husband.

—As told to *Tejeesh N.S. Behl*

Rama Prasad Goenka

Chairman Emeritus, RPG Group

In India, we have the habit of giving advice even when it is not asked. So I cannot count the number of good counsels I have received. They must be in the hundreds and thousands. I think the best advice I received was from my grandfather in 1951. My education was over and I was supposed to enter business. Father had taken some interest in Duncan Brothers and I was to go there and join it. So the first day I was to go to Duncan Brothers, as was usual in the morning, I went to my grandfather, Sir Badridas Goenka, to do my *pranam*. He said, 'So you are joining business from today!'

I said, 'Yes.'

He said, 'Remember three things. One, a written agreement can be negated by another lawyer, but what you speak, what you utter, what your lips say... *that* nobody can dismiss. Two, never hide anything from your doctor. Three, be 100 per cent honest with your lawyer.'

Years later, he said, 'I have something to add: be honest with your bankers.' I have followed this guidance and have gained immensely.

—As told to *Somnath Dasgupta*

Jignesh Shah

Chairman and Group CEO,
Financial Technologies (India) Ltd;
Vice Chairman, MCX Ltd

At the age of twenty-four, after finishing my engineering from Mumbai University, I joined the Bombay Stock Exchange, where I was part of a team responsible for designing and implementing the online trading platform. We were all young engineering graduates working overtime to understand the outcry trading systems and to devise a plan for screen-based trading.

I vividly remember that at the BSE's Phiroze Jeejeebhoy Towers, there was a huge processing room where we would often end up spending a lot of our time. One day, I came across a very old signboard, which must have been around forty to forty-five years old, that read: 'Results matter, not the efforts.' These words shook me from the core. I realized that howsoever hard you may work and whatever extra effort you may put into your work, what mattered ultimately was the outcome. Hard work is nullified if not accompanied by results. In fact, having a result-oriented approach became my mantra in life from that day. If you look around and see successful professionals or entrepreneurs, it's the result-oriented approach that differentiates them from the rest.

The second piece of advice came from the former MD of the National Stock Exchange (NSE), R.H. Patil. I was thirty-seven then. The commodity bourse, MCX, which FTIL promoted, was in direct competition with NCDEX, an exchange promoted by leading institutions like NSE, LIC, NABARD and other domestic institutions. I knew Patil from my early struggling days when he gave us (FTIL) a break as a vendor for the securities trading platform. I was a bit upset with NCDEX's ways of doing business. One day I went to meet Patil to tell him about some of the practices the competitor was resorting to in the market.

Patil advised me: 'Just don't deviate from your plan of action. Continue doing the right thing, the way you are doing now. One day, the world will notice.' Patil's encouraging words solidified my belief in not compromising on my principles and helped me stay focussed on my plan. The rest is history. In a short span of time, MCX not only overtook NCDEX in terms of market share, but now figures amongst the world's top ten commodity exchanges.

—As told to *Anand Adhikari*

R. Seshasayee

MD, Ashok Leyland

The best advice I got was from R.K. Talwar, former chairman of State Bank of India and IDBI, who set extremely high standards, both in his personal and professional life—someone whom I consider to be a giant in moral stature.

It was the early 1990s. I was in a dilemma involving a moral conflict of interest and was finding it difficult to decide what was right or wrong. Mr Talwar was then the chairman of Ashok Leyland Finance and I sought his counsel. His response was simple: 'Whichever decision will give you peace of mind and help you go to sleep peacefully is the right decision. Listen to your conscience. Most often, we put on ear plugs and don't listen to our inner voice.' Since then, all my decisions have been based on what my conscience says is right, be it taking a stand, speaking my mind, or dealing with employees and the government.

—As told to *N. Madhavan*

Anand G. Mahindra

Vice Chairman and MD,
Mahindra & Mahindra Ltd

In 1984, I had completed three years of work at Mahindra Ugine Steel after returning from business school in Boston. I was assisting in bids for large government contracts, and had worked hard on a particular initiative where we lost to a competitor on less-than-transparent grounds.

I was extremely demoralized and recall spending an evening complaining bitterly to my late father-in-law, Premnath Khandelwal, head of the eponymous group. I told him that I was contemplating returning to the US, since we at the Mahindra Group seemed to be playing according to the conventional rules of the game while success in India seemed to require following a completely different set of 'rules'.

I vividly remember that he listened patiently and let me vent my ire, and then said, 'Anand, you would be making a big mistake if you quit now. Let me tell you that your family tradition is worth upholding… because it's the right thing to do… and also because in the long run, you will enjoy a lower cost of doing business in every sense of the word.'

Since that day, I've never had any doubt about why we do business the way we do. I must add that we've never found that approach an impediment to succeeding in the areas where we chose to compete.

Vikram Kirloskar

Vice Chairman, Toyota Kirloskar Motors Ltd

After I passed out of MIT in the US in May 1981, I joined Cummins Engine Company there as an engineer. Irwin Miller, its owner, gave me an advice he routinely gave others: 'At some point, as you go through life, you may have to take a decision that may affect your career or your family. You should keep your family priorities ahead of everything else.'

As a twenty-two-year-old, I was enjoying my days at Cummins. One day, my grandfather, S.L. Kirloskar, who was on a visit to the US, asked me not to miss my cousin's wedding in India, and after that, to stay back forever and involve myself in the family business. Mr Miller's advice came handy as I chose my family. I now tell my staff members that they cannot perform well in office unless they have settled their family issues.

I received another equally powerful advice from my grandfather who advised all of us in the family that if we ever had to choose between business profits and business ethics, we must stick to the latter. This approach, at times, did not benefit our business during the pre-reform days, but paid off handsomely later. Our partnership with Toyota has been very fruitful since the relationship is built on ethics and mutual trust.

—As told to *K.R. Balasubramanyam*

Lord Swraj Paul

Founder, Caparo Group

Lots of things go back to one's early experiences. I lost my parents much too early in life, but in the time they were with me, my mother taught me the value of family and my father taught me that there is dignity in work. His office was on the ground floor while we lived on the first floor and the factory was in the backyard. At that young age he would make us sweep his office. That education has come in handier than anything else that I can think of. And you can't build a successful business without a successful family.

At the Massachusetts Institute of Technology, I learnt never to compromise on quality and to aspire for excellence. From Mrs Indira Gandhi, I learnt courage in adversity. When she lost in 1977, she remained the same person that she was earlier. I have been lucky to have learnt from many other people that I have met during my life.

—As told to *Shalini S. Dagar*

Aditya Puri

Managing Director, HDFC Bank Ltd

The best advice I ever got was from my grandfather, who was a lawyer during pre-Independence days. I was just starting out in Punjab University when my grandfather said to me: 'What you need to know first is what you really want from life.' Those words made an enormous impact on my life and got me thinking about what I really wanted from life all over again.

If you remember, those were the days when every boy wanted to be an engineer, IAS officer or a doctor. There were no other options. But I decided to pursue a degree in commerce, though my parents resented my choice. That's the one decision I took after much thought. I firmly believe that if you let other people decide for you, you cannot reach anywhere.

I wanted to be happy. That's something I was very clear about once I started working. I didn't want to be at the top of my profession. I simply wanted to be well-respected. But I also didn't want this to be the be-all and end-all of my life. I wanted a balanced life, with enough time with my family. I also needed time to follow my other hobbies such as gardening, hiking, golfing, etc. I was clear on one point—that if anything was to create conflict and affect my feeling of fulfilment, I would just give it up. Fortunately, I got support from my family. I started as an accountant, moved to Citibank as its CEO in Malaysia and again headed home to start a private sector bank from scratch.

There is another lesson that I learnt: that in the journey of your life and work, nobody can help you beyond a point. Everybody is an individual and there has to be some self-realization. Nobody can make you happy or unhappy other than yourself. Once you know what you want, it becomes very easy to navigate your way. There will always be people or family guiding you.

I often ask myself what I want to be known as. Do I want to be known as Mr Puri, who works hard day in and day out, networks, flies out and in, and whose child says he doesn't know him? Not really! I don't want to take a pot shot at anybody. Today, a lot of people, in retrospect, want to give their views about how they reached the positions they are occupying and what they did to reach those heights. I think all you can do is work hard and work with integrity.

I would be lying if I told you that I always wanted to be the MD. I did want to be. If it happened, well and good, and if it didn't, well and good too. But all this business about planning a career graph doesn't work. It's a bit like being on a boat in a river—you make the course as you go along. At all points, you face your share of obstacles and proceed further.

I must say, I have learnt at every stage of my life. I have also seen that today's youngsters take life more seriously. In fact, they are living in a brilliant time. There are opportunities everywhere. They can really contribute to the country and to the world. I would love to start all over again.

—As told to *Anand Adhikari*

Vinita Bali

Managing Director, Britannia Industries

The best advice I ever got was from an aunt who said, 'Don't give unsolicited advice to anyone, because they will ignore it anyway.' I have learnt over the years that advice has selective traction—works best with those who are ready to receive it and do something with it.

—As told to *Rahul Sachitanand*

R. Gopalakrishnan

Executive Director, Tata Sons Ltd

It is in the first ten years after one's working career begins that the greatest neglect of youthful health begins. These early years are the ones to watch. You can convince yourself about the excuses—no time to exercise, the importance of socializing, the difficulty of getting a club membership, timings and logistics problems, and a whole host of reasons. However, there are no good enough reasons for lack of fitness and exercise, other than indulgence or laziness.

While growing up in Calcutta, I joined a tennis coaching scheme at the Bengal Lawn Tennis Association. It was run and supervised by Dilip Bose, the Indian Davis Cup tennis star of the 1940s. He was a fitness fiend. Before we could get our tiny hands around the racket, he would make us run around the South Club tennis courts ten times, do 100 jumps with a skipping rope, and do another fifty sit-ups. His view was that we could not be tennis players if we were not fit.

One day, he asked us, 'How would you take care of your car if you were told that it was the only car you would have for your whole life?' The answer was quite evident and all of us kids answered in unison that we will take good care of it. 'Well, your body is the only car you will have for all your life. You cannot change it, so look after it like your only car,' he bellowed.

To a kid, that was a simple message to understand and to remember. I owe it to the late Dilip Bose that I grew to love exercise and tennis, both of which have been inexhaustible sources of pleasure, relaxation, character-building and fitness, all rolled into one.

A management career is extremely stressful, and every young executive should work at managing that stress. Some are unlucky because they develop health problems without bringing it upon themselves. But others squander away their good health on the grounds that office work is stressful. Healthy and young people should never develop stressful social habits, deluding themselves that those habits are relaxing.

Go out and enjoy life; youth comes only once. However, do listen to what your body is telling you and do not flog it to capacity. Your good health is an asset on your balance sheet. Let it grow and maintain it, but do not destroy it. It is the only opening balance of asset you get at the beginning of your life.

★

There is another piece of advice that I would like to share. Quite often, the realization that it was a coaching experience dawns on the protégé many years later. I had such an experience in Hindustan Lever.

Prakash Tandon was the legendary chairman of Hindustan Lever when I joined as a trainee. He had established a practice of inviting the trainees to lunch once a year or so. It was a terrifying experience for the trainees, but for him, it was probably a way of keeping in touch with the new recruits and getting to understand their aspirations.

On one such occasion, one of my trainee colleagues became rather expansive. Prakash Tandon said in his measured, clipped accent, 'Young men, your ears have twice the surface area of your mouth. And you have two ears as against only one mouth. So, it is good to listen four times as much as you speak.'

The temporary consequences of this devastating rebuke apart, that bit of advice has stayed with me ever after: Always keep your ears and mind open.

Whether Mr Tandon intended to mentor or not I cannot tell, but I felt mentored.

Harsh Goenka

Chairman, RPG Enterprises

If I could single out one outstanding piece of advice, it would be one that I got while reading the *Bhagwad Gita*: 'You have a right to your actions, but never to the fruits of your actions…. Self-possessed, resolute, act without any thought of results, open to success or failure.'

It was a mindset-altering piece of advice. I feel that this is the essence of a true, committed action. What it does is to liberate your thoughts and your conviction from the endless possibilities of end results. As a result, your confidence to deal with the subject remains strong, objective and independent.

When I first read it, I was a young executive in the midst of a business negotiation that was of high significance to our business. I was determined to wrest control of the direction it was taking and to achieve my objective. Obviously, it was difficult and stressful because any other outcome was just not acceptable to me. Appropriate in the very timing of its reading, this phrase struck a deep chord, and reflecting on it brought a whole new perspective. Though very difficult to put into practice, I decided to use it for my current dilemma, and amazingly, the result exceeded my expectations!

Ever since, whenever I find myself at a crossroads over a significant decision, I take the path suggested by the *Bhagwad Gita*.

—As told to *Suman Layak*

Dr Devi Shetty

Chairman, Narayana Hrudayalaya

It was some time in 1990 when I was working at B.M. Birla Heart Research Centre in Calcutta. Mother Teresa had suffered a heart attack, and I was the doctor attending to her. It turned out to be an interaction with the divine. With her, I experienced the feeling of seeing God in flesh and blood. The best advice that I ever got was from her. She said, 'Hands that help are holier than lips that pray.' These worlds left an imprint on me.

Today, everything that we do at Narayana Hrudayalaya revolves around what she had said—helping people. All our business models centre on that aim. We realize that we are part of a critical industry. Nothing will happen to you if you don't buy a house or a car today. But if you leave a major health problem unattended, it can cost you your life. In India, there is this vast majority who either can't pay or can pay only partially to access healthcare. That's why we have packages that suit every pocket. Those who can't afford it get medical treatment for free.

—As told to *K.R. Balasubramanyam*

Venugopal N. Dhoot

Chairman, Videocon Industries

In 1997, Venugopal N. Dhoot, along with one of his friends, was searching for the latter's lost son in Kolkata when he came in touch with the Missionaries of Charity, founded by Mother Teresa, which found and rescued the child. Dhoot and his friend were so impressed with the organization that they wanted to meet Mother Teresa and help the charity. During the meeting, Mother Teresa said to him, 'Live and let live,' by which she meant that people should help others. That piece of advice touched Dhoot so much that it changed his approach towards life. The advice was also similar to his guru Dongre Maharaj's teachings. Moreover,

Mother Teresa said that one is remembered for what one does for the society.

The life-altering advice had such an impact on Dhoot that within one year, he started a hospital under the name of his father Nandlal Dhoot in Aurangabad, Maharashtra. He invested Rs 200 crores of his personal and family money on building this hospital in which the poor are treated free of cost. Dhoot went on to start a school for girls on the outskirts of Aurangabad, providing free education. Nearly 2500 girls have been educated so far.

'You have to help the poor and needy with interest and affection,' says Dhoot. He says that this radical change in his thinking came when he went to Mother Teresa's charity where everybody was treated on an equal footing.

Dhoot believes that the path shown by Mother Teresa has brought her lot of praise internationally, despite her not being the head of a country or company, because of her outstanding efforts to help the needy. 'Whatever wealth one creates will remain here, but one's name will remain forever,' says Dhoot, who features on the list of richest Indians.

—Written by *Virendra Verma*

Captain G.R. Gopinath

Chairman and MD, Deccan 360

My father, the late Ramaswamy Iyengar, a farmer and a school teacher in Gorur, Karnataka, never sent me to school till I was ten. I began my first day in school from fifth standard in Kannada medium. I used to walk barefoot to school. He knew that the kind of schools that we had were regimented, and so he wanted me to lose myself in the midst of nature, the fields and the rivers, as much as I could. He repeatedly told me to have total *shraddha* (involvement, devotion) in whatever I do. That was the overarching philosophy that he imparted to me.

We were a lower middle class family, but my

father always showed me those who were less fortunate than us. He would tell me how, in spite of misery, poor labourers worked hard and led a life of contentment, and would chide me on how I, at times, complained about small things though I received so much attention and care. In hindsight, though my childhood was one of poverty, it was full of cheer and sunshine because there was no envy. My father would point to the poor to infuse happiness and contentment in me, even as he read out Tagore, Tilak, Gandhi and Socrates to enable me to have dreams and ambition.

After I left the Army in 1979, I faced many difficulties, including financial ones when banks refused to lend me money for my businesses. Similar difficulties arose when I was running helicopter and airline companies. But I always immersed myself in action, be it farming, milking cows or running my companies. Whatever I do, everything begins and ends with me losing myself in action, not in despair, cynicism or frustration. Wealth is never my destination. When a person loses oneself in *shraddha*, wealth and happiness follow.

—As told to *K.R. Balasubramanyam*

Dr A.P.J. Abdul Kalam

Former President of India

There are many pieces of advice I have received in my life which have been of immense benefit. One of the most moving ones came in October 1999 when I went to the Adhyatma Sadhna Kendra, Mehrauli. This was a year and a half after the Pokhran II nuclear tests in May 1998. The euphoria of having conducted the nuclear tests after dodging the watchful eyes of the rest of the world had far from died down.

There I met Acharya Mahapragya for the first time. After praying for the well-being of the nation with his Jain monks, he turned and blessed me. Then he uttered the words which were to change my life and my ambitions forever. He said, 'Kalam, the Almighty has a bigger mission for you and that is why you are here with me today. I know our country is a nuclear nation now. But your mission is greater than what you and your team have done; it is indeed greater than what any human being has ever done. Nuclear weapons are proliferating in tens and thousands in the world. I command you and you only with all the divine blessings at my disposal to evolve a system of peace wherein these very nuclear weapons will be ineffective, insignificant and politically inconsequential.'

The power that lay hidden behind this simple, eloquent speech left me dumbfounded. In fact, a hush fell over the hall. The realization that my work would be fruitful only if I tried to prevent the use of what I had created gave a new meaning to my life. Since then, my mission in life has been to try and contribute to peace and happiness around the world—to ensure that the fruit of my toil would not be put to use, ever.

—Adapted from The Family and the Nation, *by Acharya Mahapragya and Dr A.P.J. Abdul Kalam,* HarperCollins Publishers *India, 2008*

Contributor Profiles

AAMIR KHAN (p. 55): A superstar who is also known as the thinking man's actor and the 'perfectionist' of the Hindi film industry. Four of his films have grossed over Rs 100 crore each in four successive years.

ADITYA PURI (p. 111): Managing director of HDFC Bank, the fastest growing and the most consistently profitable bank in India.

AKHIL GUPTA (p. 61): Senior managing director of the Blackstone Group, a leading investment and advisory firm, and chairman of Blackstone India.

ALOK KEJRIWAL (p. 1): Founder and CEO of Contests2win, a leading player in the online entertainment segment in India.

ANAND G. MAHINDRA (p. 105): Vice chairman and managing director of Mahindra & Mahindra Limited, the flagship company of the $6.3 billion Mahindra Group, which features among the largest industrial houses in India.

ANU AGA (p. 96): After retiring as the chairperson of Thermax, she has been serving as the director of the $800 million company that provides a range of engineering solutions to the energy and environment sectors.

DR A. P. J. ABDUL KALAM (p. 128): He played a key role in the development of India's first satellite launch vehicle, the SLV-3, and in its missile systems. He transformed the office of the President of India during his tenure from 2002 to 2007, making it a very approachable and people-friendly institution.

ASHISH DHAWAN (p. 25): Co-founder and senior managing director of ChrysCapital Investment Advisors, which manages $2.25 billion across five funds and is a leading investment firm focussed on India.

ASHOK SOOTA (p. 10): Co-founder and executive chairman of Mindtree, one of the most reputed IT and R&D services companies in India. He has also been the president of the Confederation of Indian Industry (CII).

AZIM PREMJI (p. 35): One of India's foremost entrepreneurs, he is the chairman of Wipro, the IT giant that is a provider of integrated business, technology and process solutions globally, and is among the world's wealthiest people.

CHETAN MAINI (p. 53): Co-founder, deputy chairman and chief technical officer of Reva Electric Car Company, one of the largest producers of eco-friendly electric cars in the world.

DEEPAK PAREKH (p. 20): He is the chairman of HDFC, India's most respected housing finance company.

DEEPAK PURI (p. 31): Chairman and managing director of Moser Baer India Limited, whose cutting-edge technologies have made it the second-largest manufacturer of optical storage media in the world.

DR DEVI SHETTY (p. 122): Chairman of Narayana Hrudayalaya, this pioneering doctor has made specialized medical care accessible to thousands of people.

GAUTAM ADANI (p. 47): Chairman of the Adani Group, one of the leading conglomerates of India that has interests in varied sectors, from infrastructural development to FMCGs.

G. MADHAVAN NAIR (p. 59): Former chairman of ISRO and chairman of the Space Commission, he is a recipient of the Padma Vibhushan.

G.M. RAO (p. 65): Founder chairman of the Rs 4800 crore GMR Group, which is engaged in providing world-class infrastructure such as airports, highways and energy stations in India.

CAPTAIN G.R. GOPINATH (p. 126): One of India's most feisty entrepreneurs, he is the founder of Deccan 360, an express transportation and logistics company. As the founder of Air Deccan, he is among those who ushered in the era of low-cost flying in India.

GURCHARAN DAS (p. 92): Former CEO, P&G India and managing director, P&G Worldwide (Strategic Planning), he is the author of the international bestseller *India Unbound* and most recently, *The Difficulty of Being Good: On the Subtle Art of Dharma*.

G.V. KRISHNA REDDY (p. 29): Chairman of the GVK Group, a diversified business house that focuses on infrastructure development.

G.V. PRASAD (p. 67): Chairman and CEO of Dr Reddy's Laboratories, he played a key role in the company's ascent to the big league of the global generics business.

HARSH GOENKA (p. 120): Chairman of RPG Enterprises, which has a presence in retail, IT and communications, entertainment, power, transmission, tyres, and life sciences.

HARSH MARIWALA (p. 70): Chairman and managing director of Marico Limited; he was instrumental in transforming the commodity-driven business into a leading consumer products and services company in the beauty and wellness segment.

JAMSHED J. IRANI (p. 57): Director with Tata Sons, he is well known in the iron and steel industry and was conferred the Padma Bhushan in 2007 for his services to trade and industry.

JAVED AKHTAR (p. 51): Well-known poet, lyricist and scriptwriter, he has been a recipient of the Padma Shri and Padma Bhushan for his contribution to Indian cinema.

JIGNESH SHAH (p. 100): Founder chairman and group CEO of Financial Technologies (India) Limited, a global leader in creating and operating technology-centric, next-generation financial markets, and non-executive vice chairman of the Multi Commodity Exchange of India.

KALPANA MORPARIA (p. 23): CEO of the Indian arm of JP Morgan, she is one of the most senior and respected bankers in India.

KARAN JOHAR (p. 12): Film director, producer and talk-show host, he is one of the most sought-after celebrities and successful film-makers in the Hindi film industry.

KIRAN MAZUMDAR-SHAW (p. 37): Known as India's 'biotech queen' for her successful foray into uncharted waters when she set up Biocon, a healthcare company that delivers innovative biopharmaceutical solutions.

KISHORE BIYANI (p. 89): Founder and group CEO of Future Group, which operates multiple companies in areas such as retail, insurance, consumer credit, capital, property management, consumer brands, logistics and retail media.

M. RAMMOHAN RAO (p. 76): Former dean of the Indian School of Business, which was ranked twelfth in the global business school rankings released by the *Financial Times*, London, in 2010.

MALVINDER MOHAN SINGH (p. 27): After selling his stake in Ranbaxy, he, along with his brother, heads the Rs 1800 crore Fortis Healthcare Group and Religare, one of the fastest growing financial services institutions in India.

M.V. SUBBIAH (p. 33): Former chairman of the $3 billion Murugappa Group, one of India's leading business conglomerates with interests in diverse areas such as engineering, abrasives, finance, general insurance, cycles, sugar and farm inputs.

N. SANKAR (p. 44): Chairman of the Sanmar Group, which deals in PVC/chlorochemicals, speciality chemicals, shipping and engineering, he has been a past president of the Associated Chambers of Commerce and Industry of India (ASSOCHAM).

NIMESH KAMPANI (p. 14): Founder chairman of JM Financial Group, an integrated financial services group, he has made pioneering contributions to the development of the Indian capital markets.

PIYUSH PANDEY (p. 40): Executive chairman and creative director, Ogilvy South Asia, one of the foremost international advertising, marketing and public relations agencies.

PRASOON JOSHI (p. 78): Chairman of McCann Erickson, he has won the Cannes Lion award for his 'thanda matlab Coca-Cola' campaign. He is also a prolific poet and lyricist.

RAGHAV BAHL (p. 75): Founder and managing director of Network 18 Group, a leading Indian media conglomerate.

RAMA PRASAD GOENKA (p. 98): Chairman Emeritus of the multi-billion-dollar RPG Group, which has more than twenty companies across eight business sectors.

RAMCHANDRA AGARWAL (p. 8): Founder chairman and managing director of Vishal Megamart, which encompasses 180 showrooms in 100 cities across twenty-four states. He has been one of the catalysts that changed the way India shops.

RASHESH SHAH (p. 4): Founder chairman and CEO of Edelweiss, a financial innovation powerhouse and an emerging investment banking and financial services companies in India.

R. GOPALAKRISHNAN (p. 116): Executive director of Tata Sons and one of India's most experienced professional managers.

R. SESHASAYEE (p. 103): Managing director of Ashok Leyland, a commercial vehicle manufacturing giant and the first Indian automobile manufacturer to obtain ISO 9002 certification.

R.C. BHARGAVA (p. 82): An experienced bureaucrat, he is the chairman of Maruti Suzuki India, the largest passenger car company in India, accounting for over 50 per cent of the domestic car market share.

SANJAY NAYAR (p. 18): Former CEO of the South Asian arm of Citigroup, the international financial behemoth with operations in consumer, corporate and investment banking, and insurance.

SHAH RUKH KHAN (p. 16): Superstar of the Hindi film industry, whose fan following around the globe is unparalleled. He also runs two production companies, Dreamz Unlimited and Red Chillies Entertainment.

SHANTANU PRAKASH (p. 42): Chairman and managing director of Educomp Solutions Limited, a globally diversified education solutions provider.

SHELLY LAZARUS (p. 73): Chairman of Ogilvy & Mather Worldwide, she was awarded the prestigious Advertising Educational Foundation's Lifetime Achievement Award in 2009 for her outstanding contributions to the industry.

LORD SWRAJ PAUL (p. 109): Founder of the $1.2 billion Caparo Group that specializes in the manufacture of steel, automotive and engineering products.

VENUGOPAL N. DHOOT (p. 124): Chairman of the Rs 20,000 crore Videocon Group, which was rated among the top 100 emerging global giants by Boston Consulting Group.

VENU SRINIVASAN (p. 63): Chairman and managing director of TVS Motor Company—the only two-wheeler company in the world to be awarded the Deming Prize, a prestigious recognition in Total Quality Management—he is also the president of the Confederation of Indian Industry (2009-10).

VIKRAM AKULA (p. 85): Chairman of SKS Microfinance, India's largest microfinance company, he has been instrumental in empowering thousands of people from the underprivileged sections by providing them collateral-free loans for income generation.

VIKRAM KIRLOSKAR (p. 107): Vice chairman, Toyota Kirloskar Motors Limited, he was responsible for bringing Toyota back to India and operationalizing the six joint ventures between Toyota and the Kirloskar group.

VINITA BALI (p. 115): Managing director of Britannia Industries, one of India's most recognized and trusted brands, she was one of the key players in doubling the beverage giant Coke's historical growth rate when she was responsible for the company's worldwide strategy.

WILLIAM P. LAUDER (p. 80): CEO of Estée Lauder Companies, the internationally known manufacturers and marketers of skin care, hair care, fragrance and make-up products.